Modern Art Museum of Fort Worth

Michael Auping

seven interviews with Tadao Ando

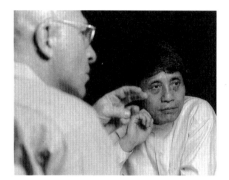

Michael Auping and Tadao Ando, May 16, 2001

Introduction

In April of 1997 Tadao Ando was selected as the design architect for the new Modern Art Museum of Fort Worth. Since that time, the architect has made numerous visits to Fort Worth to meet with the Museum's Building Committee and staff to discuss the design of the new museum. Following one of those meetings, I asked him if on his next visit he would set aside some time for a brief interview. Seven interviews followed over a period of four years. My original motive was simply to talk about the Fort Worth project. The architect immediately expanded that focus to include topics ranging from children, students, boxing, Zen, and the Pantheon to the making of concrete, Louis Kahn, darkness, tatami mats, and postmodernism, among others.

As should be clear from these discussions, I am not an architectural historian. At best, I am an enthusiastic student, and the following dialogues are presented in the spirit of offering those of us who are interested in Mr. Ando's buildings, but are not architectural specialists, a foundation or introduction to his philosophy. One of the most impressive aspects of that philosophy is his insistence that architecture is not a complex of stylistic strategies, but a basic expression of consciousness; or as Le Corbusier (after whom Ando named his late and beloved dog) said, a deep reflection of "civilization itself." Ando's spare references to architectural history are couched in the practical understanding of basic human needs and how the respectful handling of materials can not only enclose but dignify space and those that inhabit it.

The need to bring an emotion or idea to material form—whether through the subtleties of drawing or the weightiness of poured concrete—is perhaps the essence of his personality. His physical character is reflected in the fact that he is continuously drawing. Throughout each interview, which took place with a translator, Mr. Ando would invariably pick up a pencil or crayon and begin marking as a means of expressing a given thought. After each discussion, I kept the sheets—no matter how cryptic—in a file folder. Many of those drawings are illustrated here. We have placed them in the proximity of where they occurred in the discussion. In some cases they may relate directly to an idea the architect was expressing. Others are more abstract and may have only an oblique relationship to the discussion. Since we could not always be sure, we have not captioned them, preferring that the readers make their own connections.

I would like to thank Junichi Uenomata, who translated the first two interviews, and Kulapat Yantrasast, who translated all of the others, and who has been a sounding board throughout the interview process. I would also like to express my gratitude to Marla Price, Director of the Modern Art Museum of Fort Worth, for her consistent support of these dialogues and their publication. Yumiko Ando and Masataka Yano have also provided helpful support, for which I am also very grateful.

Most of all, I want to thank Mr. Ando, who has been exceptionally patient and has enriched my knowledge of architecture and the creative process in so many ways. I hope that those who read these interviews will be able to get a glimpse of the man and his architecture as I have been fortunate to do over the past four years.

Michael Auping

May 13, 1998

Michael Auping: Were you interested in buildings when you were young?

Tadao Ando: As a child, I used to go looking at the construction sites near my home in Osaka. I always thought the carpenters were important people. They looked so great for me, a young boy with so much interest toward making things by my own hands. They would put the frames up before the siding was put on, and they were so confident and proud that the house they were building would stand for 100 years. I was very impressed by that as a child. They would tell me that a building must be built with confidence and pride—materials alone do not make a building great or strong. Becoming an architect, or any profession, is usually gradual. You don't know exactly when you become that person who is an architect, but I think that maybe it was that moment for me that I could imagine myself as a builder. The combined effect of beginning to understand a carpenter's confidence, and the pride of a craftsman, made me think that this could be a way for me to contribute to society in some way.

MA: What type of a house did you grow up in?

TA: We all have had certain experiences in our childhood that have stayed with us for our entire lives. The house that I grew up in was very important for me. It is an old Japanese small wooden house partitioned into several units—a Nagaya row house. It is very long, and when you come in from the street you walk through a corridor and then into a small courtyard and then another long space that takes you deeper into the house. The courtyard is very important because the house is very long and the amount of light is very limited. Light is very precious. When you live in a space like that you realize how important light is to interior space. Living in a space like that, where light and darkness are constantly interacting, was a critical experience for me.

MA: You can see that in your buildings, in the sense that you pass through various intensities of light that create different moods in each space. You also

create long walls that catch light, natural light, and that change throughout the day. Do you think these characteristics refer back to that house?

TA: Yes, but it's unconscious and very natural for me. The memory of that house has always stayed with me, the ways the rooms seemed to be painted in shadow and light. That is how I experience space. When I was fifteen years old I took part in renovating that house. I knew the house so well, and the workers and craftsmen let me join them. It was a very important learning experience. I was very proud that I could contribute because I knew the house very well. By working with them side by side, I developed an intimacy with that project that was very important for me.

MA: Was it a well-built house?

TA: It was a very common, typical house that was built about ten to fifteen years before the second World War. The house was sixty-five to seventy years old at the time when we renovated it. There are many houses like it in Japan. So in that sense there wouldn't appear to be anything special about the house. It was in a working-class neighborhood. Across the street was a craftsman's small factory that did a lot of wood works and next door was a shop that did a lot of small stone works, especially used for the Japanese chess games. So I grew up in this neighborhood watching all these people working with their hands. It made me very conscious of how things were made and built, and the joy that could come from making something with your hands. I was very lucky to have that. At the same time, I also remember the strange fact that you had to sell what you made because it is your occupation. I remember seeing that as a very difficult moment for the craftsmen, that they had created something and they didn't want to let it go, but of course they had to. What they had left was the sense of pride that this thing could go out into the world and maybe affect it in some small way. I certainly understand those feelings now. The house and neighborhood where I grew up shaped how I see things. Those craftsmen in my neighbor-hood shaped how I feel about making things. I always felt that neighborhood shaped my eyes and my heart. They are the kind of people who are so busy living and building that they made building a joyful thing. Building something was not a problem for them but a life itself.

MA: It seems those childhood experiences precede and form how we educate ourselves, because education is not a set experience for everyone.

Certainly you have taken an unusual course in being essentially self-taught, rather than following a typical university training.

TA: I'm sure every architect has a story to tell and that story is the beginning of one's path. For example, Mies van der Rohe's father was a stonemason and his experience at a very young age of seeing his father work affected his approach to life and his profession. Louis Kahn's parents were artists; his father a musician and his mother a painter. Le Corbusier's father was a watchmaker and his first teacher was a painter. So he learned to use his hands and eyes in a certain way. It's this kind of learning that leads you into a profession naturally.

MA: It's experiential rather than theoretical.

TA: Yes. That is how it works for me.

MA: Do you remember any other buildings as a child?

TA: I also have a very strong image from my childhood of the farmhouses. The Japanese farmhouse is very unpretentious. There is something so honest about how they look with their over-protecting roof and how they function as a place of protection. The way they withstand the weather and stand so strongly in the landscape—I think they have a very powerful presence. And the way the *engawa*[1] is employed in those buildings is very strong. When you talked a while ago about how much you appreciate the experience of Ryoanji, the rock garden, I was thinking to myself that the most interesting part of experiencing Ryoanji for me is the building that faces the garden, and particularly the floor of the *engawa* that faces the garden, the way the light falls down onto the floor of that transitional space, that *engawa*. It engages the space of the rocks without intruding on it. It sets the stage for seeing the rocks.

MA: That's an important boundary, and one that obviously comes into play in the design of a museum.

TA: Architecture has always been about boundaries; building boundaries for protection and then opening them up for movement.

---

1 *Engawa* is the narrow, enclosed space in a traditional Japanese building that serves as a transition between a room and the outside environment; similar to a Western porch or veranda.

MA: As a young man when you began traveling to look at architecture as a means of self-training, what were some of the first buildings that impressed you?

TA: In my early twenties I traveled all around Japan. In Hiroshima, I saw Kenzo Tange's Peace Center.[2] It is a concrete building supported by *pilotis*. That left me with a very strong image. I think that was partly because it was in Hiroshima. It was something about the strength of the building and the history of the place. The place talks about the possibilities of humankind, and the strength of people to survive. The architecture also spoke of that kind of strength. I think I felt at the time that architecture should have a responsibility to speak to the strengths of humankind in the same way that men should have a responsibility to other men. In this way, architecture plays a moral role in our life. It is an inspiration; at the same time it is a protection.

MA: Then you traveled outside of Japan to see the Pantheon and the Parthenon.

TA: It was very important for me to travel to these buildings, not to study them in an academic sense but to see them, be in them, experience them as a form. In Japan, when you study architecture, you are basically studying Western architecture. With that in mind, I felt I needed to go to the source of Western architecture, which is Greek and Roman architecture. So when I started my journey, I visited the Pantheon and the Parthenon. I still believe those buildings to be a great source for the architecture that followed them. When I design a building, those images are always with me. I design according to function and the site that is presented to me, but within that I always go back to thinking about those buildings and their effect as a built structure.

MA: You also went to Africa.

TA: In Morocco, I went to see Caspar. I remember thinking when I saw it from afar that it looked like this very chaotic, out-of-order settlement. But when you actually enter, you realize the sense of order in that place. What creates that order is the lifestyle of the people, the social order that has developed based on the geography they inhabit. I was very interested in the cliff dwellings that were set within this fairly drastic topography. The cave

2 Kenzo Tange designed the Peace Center in 1952. This is a memorial building for praying for eternal peace, commemorating the atomic bombs dropped during World War II.

is such a basic form of protection, and that is a basic priority of architecture, and related to social order.

MA: Le Corbusier said that architecture is "civilization itself"; in other words, the ultimate form of social sculpture.

TA: I agree with that. Architectural form reflects and directs how we relate to ourselves, to each other, to nature, to materials. Look at the small island of Japan and the spaces that are created there with wood and paper, and compare that to the United States or Germany. All of these architectures reflect the place and the cultures that have learned to inhabit the specific requirements of their land. The challenge that they all have in common is protecting the individual as well as society, and then creating an environment that brings them together as a society.

MA: It must be intimidating to think of what a broad discipline architecture is.

TA: For me it is a way of participating in society.

MA: You are an unusual case in that you are self-educated, with no university education. How did you actually enter the field of architecture?

TA: I began as a craftsman and a builder, working with my hands. I still miss that now. Working with your hands and muscles is important. It is very important, very important to understand scale and weight, and the voice of materials. I don't want to design impractical things that a human being cannot build. Working with your hands teaches you very basic concepts of beauty. For example, I like concrete because it is handmade compared to some other types of modern building methods.

MA: Is there a point when you recognize that you are going from being a builder to being an architect? Do you remember acknowledging that stage in your life?

TA: It was a gradual process. It did not happen at a fixed moment. The period when I decided to travel around Europe in 1965 was critical. I saw the Parthenon in Greece, the Pantheon in Rome, and many works of Le Corbusier. That was when I knew that architecture could be a creative force, that a building represented something more than a protection from the weather. That took me to a higher level of thinking about architecture.

MA: As a young man you were also a boxer, semi-professional. Assuming that we learn something from everything, is there anything you learned as a boxer that has helped you with your architecture? They seem like strange bedfellows, one so much about motion and violence, the other still and classical.

TA: They are of two different worlds—architecture in the realm of the creative and boxing in the realm of the purely physical. The one thing I can say is that in boxing you have to be courageous and take some chances, always taking one step deeper into your opponent's side. You must risk moving into a dangerous area in order to fully take advantage of your skills and eventually win the match. Creating something in architecture—not just building something but creating something—also requires courage and risk, moving into areas that are not so known, taking that extra step forward. If you stay in your day-to-day lifestyle, just building buildings without thinking about why you build buildings and never questioning yourself, it doesn't require courage. To create a form of architecture, something that may not look familiar, you have to take that extra step into the unknown.

MA: Is the element of balance also something they have in common, both requiring a kind of physical and visual balance?

TA: Of course balance is important, but to win you have to move forward boldly, and forget about your balance for a moment, only hoping that you naturally have balance as you strike forward. There are many good buildings with balance, but that does not necessarily mean they are creative buildings. They are buildings with no problems, but no questions either. To make creative architecture you have to take one more step forward, and then you make problems and maybe some important questions, too. Then, as an architect, you have to solve the problems and answer the questions in order to complete the move forward. In boxing you must finish the move in order to win.

For example, this Fort Worth museum is different from buildings I have built before. If I were to make the same building like I have made before, it doesn't require any courage or risk. In this case, I'm trying to do something new. It is a double structure with concrete volumes encased in a glass-skin box. It is unusual and it is a risk I take because it's not so easy to build and there is not much tolerance for error in terms of craftsmanship. It is particularly important to take steps forward in a museum building for contemporary

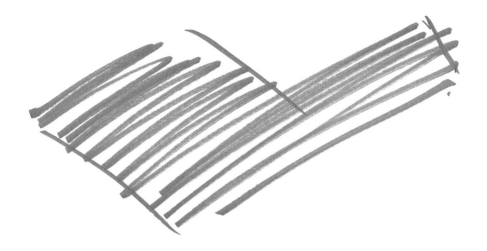

art. The living artists are very courageous. They are stepping forward all of the time. We must meet them moving ahead. We must share the fear of challenging the unforeseen world. We are all humans and we can be courageous, but we cannot escape the fear when you take risks. Fear is a way to measure our abilities, to understand the fear and solve the problems without being reckless. As long as you have courage to step forward, and some experience, you are not likely to fail.

MA: You've done a number of projects that have been risky in technical terms, in Mount Rokko and Awaji Island.

TA: The Mount Rokko complex in Kobe is a stepped housing project built into the hills. On Awaji Island, I made a Buddhist temple beneath a pond, which is called Water Temple. Both projects sit on very active fault lines. I knew I was doing something risky, but I knew it could be done—make something that looked dignified and that had the strength to stay there. Although they are located in the midst of the disaster-stricken area, they did survive the Kobe earthquake. The temple underneath the pond is tensioned with piano wire. The Rokko Housing is tied down to the rock bed with the earth as anchor. I'm very proud of those projects. I'm very proud of their strength.

MA: What are some of the other aspects of the Fort Worth project, besides the double skin, that you see as courageous or daring?

TA: There is an image I have in mind that is not typical of any of my buildings. I envision this building as a swan floating on the water. From a distance, it is the image I think you will see. To make a building look like a swan is not an easy job. [laughter] But it is not impossible. It has been done before. There is a famous temple in Kyoto, Byodo-in Temple in Uji. It looks like a phoenix, a legendary swan that is a reflection in the water. The Fort Worth project is part of this image. When the Fort Worth building is lighted from the inside and its form is united with the reflection on the pond, it will make a very beautiful image.

Of course, a building is not just about a shape. You have to give people an experience of space. People will be able to see the art in an intimate way, but also there will be spaces that combine inside and outside, nature and art. You can be one with nature, looking out over the pond away from the art or inside toward the art. In some cases art and nature will share the space. This is unusual I think. The glass and the water make this a very unique space.

You will always be aware of nature in this building. I think of it as an arbor for art. I don't think there are many art museums like this in the world. I have not seen any. This is all made possible by this unique site. We can build the natural into and around the building and situate the building correctly to take advantage of every viewpoint and the movement of light. This building is about serenity, and we have to be very careful to allow this serenity to grow from the building and its site. It's a hard thing to achieve.

MA: It sounds like a very Japanese concept for a public building.

TA: I think so.

MA: Japanese architecture has a long and distinguished history, and modern architecture, it seems to me, has a separate history. One involves a kind of sacred space; the other, a secular one. Would it be fair to say that you are trying to bring these two separate histories together?

TA: Here in Fort Worth, yes.

MA: What about in general? Don't all of your buildings do this in some way?

TA: The art museum, like the church, creates a special space in people's lives. Day-to-day life is very busy, very hectic. At the museum, although it is an extension of your life, you are allowed, by facing the art and the environment, to reclaim yourself. If you can be with yourself and your thoughts in a serene place for even just one hour, then this space can provide a special point of energy. I don't want people to come to be entertained, but to come to reclaim and nourish their spirit and soul. That is the place I want to build. So, I see the ideal space as being both sacred and secular, to allow the individual either possibility through the serene openness of the place. For me, I like to think about being in a space that allows you to forget about the secular side of life, and focus on yourself, which is the sacred. Maybe I am too philosophical today, but when I talk about the individual and the space, I am talking about approaching the space of the cosmos. Even if the space is small there can be the potential of the cosmos. If the space is constructed with a forceful imagination, there is the possibility of entering the space and leaving it at the same time.

MA: So from your point of view, the universe is inside the individual and the architectural space turns in on the individual. It's not an illustration of an outward space. The space, if properly constructed, is always a reflection of something inside you.

TA: Yes. The universe, of course, has many faces. It is the basis of aesthetics, of harmony and balance. The universe is the future and the past. So an architecture that can approach these conditions becomes more than just a building. This is a Japanese kind of thinking, which is not so much American. I think what you say is true, that Japanese buildings, the best ones, work toward a sacred space and the best American buildings have a strong secular space. This is not always true, but in general, I think.

MA: When you approach a site, what elements or characteristics do you look for that determine how you will build? What features tend to inspire you?

TA: The architecture should have its own universe, but as you say, the architecture should feel the strengths and the force of the site. It is always more complicated than our theories. In an urban site, one has to be practical and the given land must address other buildings and walkways, how people move. In an open site like Fort Worth, the land suggests a placement that has mostly to do with the topographic energy of the land itself. This site has a green forest, the potential for an arbor within a city. This will establish it as a strong but peaceful force in a fairly busy city area. There is also a collective sort of universe created by the team members—the architecture team, the funding team, the museum staff. Everyone has to believe that something can be achieved on that site. It is not simply a matter of building a building. Anyone with money can make buildings. However, there must be a quality of hope and belief—that is one of the most important elements of creative architecture. The cost of a project, of course, is important, but it is not the most important. This morning I saw the test concrete mock-up wall built by your construction consultant, Linbeck. I think they achieved very good workmanship. Working with them, I'm sure we can build better concrete than you typically see. We can build the quality of work against which all other concrete structures will be measured. By doing so, encased in glass, and reflected on the pond, you will see a swan.

MA: The vocabulary of forms you use seems very basic: the square, the rectangle, and a kind of circle or ellipse, which particularly fascinates me.

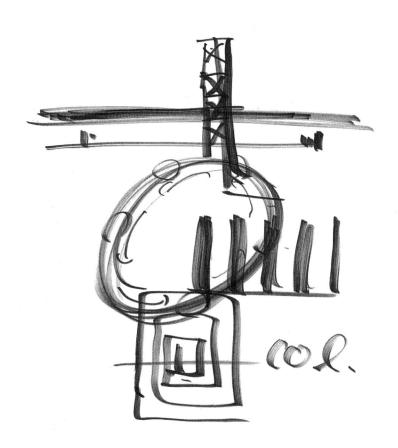

I can see it in modernist terms—Le Corbusier incorporated curves, and Frank Lloyd Wright, among others I probably am not thinking of; Louis Kahn's vaulted roofs at the Kimbell, for that matter. But your use of the curve is somehow different. It is often a half circle.

TA: Are you familiar with Zen?

MA: Somewhat.

TA: The essence of Zen philosophy is a circle. The circle, of course, represents infinity. When you are talking about my curves, you are talking about maybe one-fourth or one-sixth of a circle as the symbol of infinity. So how you connect the rest of the circle to make your universe is up to your own mind. I try to achieve the possibility of that completion in the mind of the viewer. You fulfill the space. A number of great buildings in the West as well as the East incorporate this concept: the Pantheon in Rome, for example. The upper half is a perfect semi-sphere. The lower half is a cylinder, both created with the same radius and height. The light penetrates through the center of the dome into the space. It is a perfect space. The scale is perfect for the human body and for the possibility of thinking about the human form in relation to the universe. When they conduct the choir in that space, the human voice resonates like a universe. At 10:00 in the morning on Sunday, they do a choir and chant. I was asked to give a lecture at the University of Rome last November, and I was able to attend Mass. That event reassured me that architecture is not just a form, not just light, not just the sound, not just the material, but the ideal integration of everything. The human element is the key that ties it all together. A great building comes alive only when someone enters it. A form is not imagination. A form brings out imagination. The Pantheon does that in a powerful way.

MA: When you received the Pritzker Prize three years ago, you chose to receive it at Versailles. I was under the impression that the award recipient can choose anywhere in the world to receive the prize. Why Versailles and not the Pantheon?

TA: Versailles was not chosen by me. I was told that the French President Chirac decided. This year, Renzo Piano was awarded the Pritzker Prize. This is the twentieth Pritzker Prize. That award will be given at the White

House. President Clinton is inviting the twenty winners for the award ceremony. I wish I could have chosen the place. That would be interesting.

MA: It seems ironic that someone who never attended a university has taught at Harvard and Yale, and now has a professorship at Tokyo University, one of the most difficult universities to be accepted into in the world. How does a self-taught architect teach a philosophy of architecture to some of the brightest university-trained students?

TA: To begin with, as you say, Tokyo University is a unique place. The students are very carefully screened through a very competitive system of learning. They come out of a system of all study and no play. Their heads are packed with as much information as is humanly possible. They are not allowed to come into the University until they have gone through this rigorous training. But accumulating information and thinking are two different things. To teach architecture to these students is to make them realize that architecture is interesting and even fun, and that knowledge does not make you a good architect. Artists like Constantin Brancusi, Henry Moore, Alberto Giacometti, Isamu Noguchi, and Richard Serra are all great thinkers. Their knowledge is tremendous, but knowledge alone did not make them great artists.

MA: So if intelligence and knowledge are not enough, what is the other part of the equation? What is the other element? Intuition?

TA: I think it could be memory, the strong memory of something that we all carry with us. Some things that we encounter, for some reason, we never forget. These memories inspire us to do some things in a certain way, to make a form or to write something that intelligence and knowledge by themselves would not produce. For those who grew up looking at the Pantheon in Rome, then the memory of that space will be with them for the rest of their lives and will affect, in some basic ways, what they do and how they do things. For me, for us in Japan, the great cities Kyoto and Nara live within us as a strong memory. Those cities and ancient buildings are with us all the time, wherever we are. We have to learn to cultivate that memory, because memory organizes our philosophy about time, space, color, politics, everything. When Frank Lloyd Wright went to Japan, that experience transformed his work, his way of looking at the world, for the rest of his life. You can also see his memories of his trips to Mexico. I carry the memory of the house I grew up in. So reading, studying, and talking is good to mature the mind, to exercise it, but you have to go out into the world and experience it. You have to have direct contact with the spaces, the materials, and with people. This is why I traveled so much before I began designing buildings. You must find out how many great memories you can accumulate. That is the only way to complete the education. It is all about making powerful memories. So this Fort Worth museum has a great responsibility. How it can leave great memories in the minds of children. It must feed them because they will make the next buildings and write the next poetry. A great memory for children is the greatest legacy we can leave. I know that you are very much aware of this responsibility. That is how you form your permanent collection and choose your exhibitions. It is the greatest responsibility a museum has.

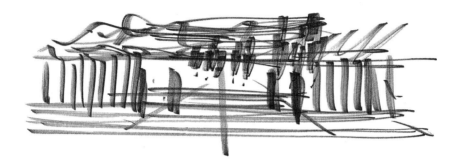

November 30, 1998

Michael Auping: I wanted to ask you a little bit more about the Fort Worth project. You have said that it is meant to suggest a specific symbol, a swan on the water. Are there other buildings that you have done that suggest such a specific symbol?

Tadao Ando: I always have an image in mind when I begin. It is a first impression. Fort Worth could be similar to the Naoshima project. In Naoshima, the image I had was to build a castle. This was the first impression I had—a castle on a hill on an island—a dream image that was accessible for people, especially for children. It was an image that I thought could inspire their imagination as soon as they saw it from the water.

In this case—I'm talking now about Fort Worth—I saw the image of a swan flying over to the site, bringing something to this place. The swan would bring something that gives birth to something larger than itself. The image of a swan floating on the water is the beginning symbol that would suggest something even more imaginative. The swan sits quietly connecting the land to a future expression. I would like to see children and their families come here, not just to see one image—the paintings or the swan image or the environment—but to experience all of it as a place to think about themselves and their own dreams.

MA: When you talk about swans and castles, it almost sounds like you are talking about a fairy tale. Do you know the term *fairy tale*?

TA: Yes, but this is not specific. Disney, for example, presents a specific fantasy. It is a very successful fantasy environment. What I am talking about is a more intellectual and philosophical type of dream. Not a place to escape yourself, but to connect with yourself.

MA: In a number of articles on your work, authors have referred to your creating a "pure space." I'm curious what you think they mean by that. It seems to me that is a contradiction, since space is never really pure; it is always filled

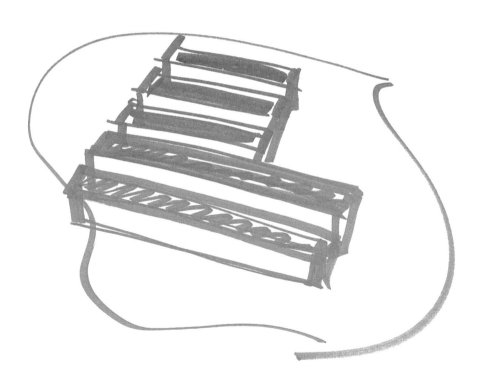

with emotion, ideas. Wouldn't this go against what you have just said? Isn't the idea of a neutral or pure space a fallacy?

TA: This is true. Space will only have a life when people enter it. So the important role architecture can play, and that space plays within that architecture, is to encourage an interaction between people, between people and the ideas being presented in the paintings and sculpture, and most importantly within people themselves. Walls, ceilings, windows should encourage ideas, and ideas are not pure. They are diverse and layered. We are sitting here, and this space is functioning to encourage this discussion. So this space is private and quiet, so it works for a primary function, which is to allow us to have a discussion. However, good architecture is not just about primary functions. You must also take into account secondary and tertiary functions, and even beyond that. A space is never about one thing. It is a place for many senses: sight, sound, touch, and the unaccountable things that happen in between. Working with space and form is about working with as much of the human intellect and spirit as possible.

MA: It sounds like your first thoughts about a building are about space— which is difficult to describe—and secondarily, the physical form of a building, which is perhaps easier to talk about.

TA: The form allows the space, gives birth to the space. There is a famous Japanese scholar, Kakuzo Okakura, who wrote a book in English about the tea ceremony titled *The Book of Tea*. Frank Lloyd Wright must have read his book, and was very impressed by his thoughts. Okakura expressed the idea that the space where the tea ceremony takes place is much more critical than a ceiling, floor, and four walls that surround the space. It is not that simple. Space is made available not simply by containment, but by expression. As I understand it, when Frank Lloyd Wright finished reading Okakura's thoughts, he said it was the first time he really understood the meaning of space. The book was written almost 100 years ago, written in English by a Japanese who lived in the Meiji Era. It must be one of the first examples of a Japanese writing in English. I can send it to you, if you like.

MA: Thank you. I would like to read it very much. Does Okakura, or do you, suggest that the creation of space is completely intuitive, or is it possible to quantify space, to in essence make a kind of formula that achieves what you want by creating a certain proportion of space?

TA: Well, it is partly intuitive, but as you know it also relates to the human body. A building should be built in response to the human body. We could say that the average height of a person is approximately 1.8 meters [5' 9"]. When you look at a tatami mat in Japan you can see that one person can lie on it. It represents the space of one person. But it is also the perfect size for two people to sit on, face to face. If you stand up a tatami, it becomes a door. So a tea ceremony house is made of proportions based on a simple tatami mat.

MA: It's like the Japanese version of the golden mean.

TA: You could say that. It is a form of measurement based on the human body. It takes into account a human presence from the very beginning.

MA: In the Fort Worth project, you are placing a concrete container inside of a glass container—in other words, a building within a building or a space within a space. The space between the concrete and the outer glass wall is like a transition space. Is this like the *engawa* you've described in some Japanese buildings?

TA: Yes. The *engawa* is a passageway or space that brings together the inside and the outside. It is psychological as much as physical. Western architecture is often thought of as a space enclosed by walls; the walls point inside. Asian architecture is more oriented to the outside; it can also be said that it is more open to nature. But today we should not think of making "Western" or "Asian" architecture, but something that is global, a bridge to a space that is about any person. If we think globally, we are thinking about expanding barriers, overcoming barriers. By using glass as a wall, physically there is a barrier, a protection from the outside, but visually there is no boundary between outside and inside. There is also the light that comes off the water and through the glass that indicates a lack of boundary and can make its presence felt on the wall. So at certain times of day you will see the movement of the water as a reflection inside the space. At the same time, the interior galleries are protected. I don't think this effect has ever been attempted. In Japan, for example, a building is placed at an elevation some sixty centimeters above the water. So reflected light is often blocked, not allowed to go inside the space. In the Fort Worth building, the difference between the surface of the water and the floor of the building is not that great. It is like a continuation of the space. So in this *engawa* there will be a sense that you are almost standing on the water and that you are inside and outside at the same time—no visual boundaries.

MA: Since you bring up the subject of light, it gives me a chance to ask about color, your attitude about color and its role in architecture. Some would say that you have a very subdued palette, given the predominance of gray concrete. This is certainly a different approach than one sees in the work of many postmodern architects, from Arata Isozaki to Frank Gehry to Rem Koolhaas.

TA: As you know, there are wide variations in color from white to gray to black. Concrete can be very rich in color. I see color there in terms of depth rather than surface. The gradations of color create a sense of depth. If you only look at color in terms of projecting out from the surface, then you fail to see the depth.

MA: Do you think this idea of color and depth relates to how one experiences space in your buildings?

TA: I think so. I am convinced that concrete implies a layering of many subtle colors, and I hope the color does not fight the space, but enhances its depth. I think this is true of fine art in general—that color is best used when it suggests depth. For example, the red of an Ellsworth Kelly has great depth. In my buildings, I also want to accommodate the quality of depth. I think this is particularly important in a museum building, where the fine art must be allowed to assert itself within the depth I provide. The kind of color you may be thinking of comes from the outside in my buildings, the color of the landscape that surrounds many of my buildings. Just the colors of nature that can enter the building through the glass—that is enough color I think. The concrete does not interfere with this process. I think it can absorb and complement nature.

MA: Can we say that concrete—its color, surface, its general presence—is your signature material?

TA: Yes, but that requires some elaboration. It is not just a matter of *my* use of concrete. The use of concrete is a historical phenomenon. As you know, at the end of the nineteenth century, so-called reinforced concrete was first used in France by Auguste Perret in an apartment building on rue Franklin. The twentieth century is the era of concrete and steel. Concrete gave the twentieth century a completely new means to express itself through architecture. It provided a new kind of freedom of expression for architecture. Before the twentieth century, buildings were mainly made with masonry.

Because of the weight and piece-by-piece construction of that kind of material, you had to be very careful where you could put a door or a window. There were not so many options because the situation was restricted by the nature of the building material. Prior to the twentieth century, the main way, sometimes the only way, an architect could express himself was through decoration, ornamentation. The form or structure of a building was not manipulated in any significant way. So when you say that concrete is my signature material, you need to understand it in this context. I am among a number of architects who use concrete because of the freedom it allows me. I like concrete because I can invent forms, which allows me to create new kinds of spaces.

MA: They say that concrete is the marble of the twentieth century.

TA: Except that marble is far more limited in what it can express in forming space.

MA: So it is an irony that some of the great architects of our time have used concrete because of its expressiveness, and yet many of the ugliest buildings in the world are now made of concrete.

TA: It is true. Concrete gives the illusion that it is easy to work with because you can pour a long wall relatively quickly rather than having to build it brick by brick. In one sense, anyone can handle it. Because of that, people often use it very casually, even carelessly. You cannot create just any form with concrete, because it also has its limitations. To use your example, concrete needs to be treated with the same respect as marble, if it is to have the same visual presence. For example, Louis Kahn, who built your neighbor the Kimbell Art Museum, understood this very well. Kahn had a deep understanding of the property of concrete.

MA: How involved are you in establishing the recipe of making the concrete mix and then in the precision of pouring it in order to get the proper surface?

TA: It's not that difficult. The recipe of course is simple: pebbles, rocks, cement, sand, and water. That's it. It does have to be mixed carefully, but this can be done without too much difficulty. You just have to choose the right amount of each. There is also the rebar, the reinforcing bar, and this is very important. The rebar is like the bones of a human body. The concrete is like the flesh. I think of a poured-concrete building as a metaphor of the human body. If you have a thick bone and not enough muscle and skin, the bone will start to stick out. Or if you have too much skin with no sense of bone, the building will look fat and bloated. It is very important to maintain the precise space, the right amount of space between the rebar. Once that spacing is established, it must be maintained precisely. In Japan, say we are doing a twenty-meter wall, then we are talking about .05 tolerance. Also, the rebar cannot come too close to the surface. If you're careful about these things, concrete can be very beautiful, very harmonious. The surface will look good; the concrete will not crack and will not be too porous. It is simply a matter of finding people who understand this. It is this simple information that in part separates a beautiful concrete wall from a concrete wall that is not so beautiful. It is so simple, but as far as I can tell very few people are doing it in the world. They don't take the time to think about it. Americans have no trouble learning the precision because they have great pride to do things the best way once they understand the goal. If you forget your pride, and it becomes just a business, you cannot make the kind of building we are talking about. Poured-in-place concrete is a kind of handmade building. It requires some attention.

MA: Is it easier to find these construction people in Japan than in America?

TA: It is the same everywhere. America and Japan both have very high standards of technology, particularly America. But that is not enough. One of the important roles of an architect is to help his engineers and workers have pride. They must see that the architect and his entire team have pride. When that is obvious then the goals become clear.

I should also point out that the twentieth century has also been the era of glass. So along with the flexibility of concrete, we have the possibility of transparency. Within that concept is visual transparency and logical transparency—transparency that involves a very clear-cut logic. I have not seen very many buildings that create a harmony between visual transparency and logical transparency of glass with concrete.

MA: I'm not sure I know what you mean.

TA: Architecture consists of two elements; an intellectual element in that we have to create a space that is logical and clear, that has a logical or intellectual order. At the same time, you have to use your senses to imbue the space with life. These are the two main aspects of creating architectural space. One is practical and theoretical; the other is sensory and intuitive. So let's look at glass. Anyone can use glass, just as anyone can use concrete. So we shouldn't look at concrete and glass as simply materials to construct a set of forms. It has to be more than that, a larger, more in-depth feeling for the space. When I draw from the architecture of Greece and Rome, especially Greece, I am trying to understand how the geometry is combined with spirit and material to make something that has a special order. When you say order, people often imagine limitations and containment, but I think of a geometry that expands to the spirit of the living person who enters the building. The order must feel expansive.

MA: It seems like a paradox: an expanding concept of space, but one that is also logical, and by that I mean a place where people do not get lost, and that they have a sense of where they are when they are in the space. There is a book I read in college titled *Keep the River on Your Right*, which is about psychological and literal navigation, that sense of going on an adventure but always knowing how to get back. How does an architect maintain this balance? For instance, how does an architect decide where to put the entrance to a building, and how does the entrance relate to what I would call the "center" of a building?

TA: First of all, the entrance, of course, is always important. It is the birth of the experience and summarizes the kind of experience you will have. Where the entrance is placed is often a practical matter of the site and traffic flow, but how it reveals the order of the building on entering is very important. In Fort Worth, because of the glass at the front and back of the entrance lobby, you see a kind of panorama of the gallery pavilions floating on the water and the enclosing forest area. When you enter this building, you understand the logic of expansiveness immediately. The gallery pavilions, the water, the landscape are all seen together at a glance.

The idea of a center is an interesting one, and one that is more of a Western concept. Roland Barthes made a comment on visiting Japan that it is a country that doesn't seem to have a center; great depth, but no center. I think I carry that aspect of Japan with me. For me, the center of a building is always the person who is in it, experiencing the space from within themselves. The challenge is in allowing each person to be the center, to be generous enough with the space to allow them to feel they are the center.

MA: When you say generous, do you mean in terms of size?

TA: Not necessarily. Some buildings are small on the outside, but very big on the inside. And the opposite is also true. I think to be generous with space is a matter of making someone comfortable enough to explore, to find their own way within the building. It's like wearing clothing. The material surroundings should give you a sense that you are covered, but not seem constricting.

MA: In trying to create these types of spaces you are talking about, what do you think is the most important tool an architect has to work with? I notice that you do a lot of hand drawings and sketches. Some architects are more comfortable at the computer. I understand that there are many tools, but is there one that for you personally is most critical?

TA: It is funny but I use my head as a tool, a place to walk around. That is where I come up with the first image of a space. The first image is always the most important to me. The first image could be a circle or a triangle, a very basic idea of a space and its relation to a site. I can see that first in my head. You can see that my sketches are very simple. In the process of working on a building, I try never to lose that first simple image. It usually embodies the very spirit of the building. From there, more specific ideas can be developed. At that point, I can use any other tools that I like to develop the idea: computer, models, etc.

MA: Do you spend much time reading?

TA: I try to find time for reading, but architecture requires constant attention.

MA: When you are not reading about architecture, what types of books do you gravitate to?

TA: I have been thinking and reading about history and philosophy recently. I have been reading through some of the lectures that I have given at Tokyo University, and I have noticed that I have been thinking about how architecture has drawn much from the field of philosophy. I think about Peter Eisenman and deconstructionism and its relationship to French philosophy. The relationship between philosophy and architectural theory interests me very much.

MA: What philosophers interest you in particular?

TA: What I have been thinking about lately is that many of the best architectural concepts could relate closely to the ideas of Martin Heidegger. I was reading a Norwegian architecture critic recently, Christian Norberg-Schulz, and he seems to think the same thing. Heidegger suggests that what architecture is about is creating a living space; a space that opens the imagination of who is in it. Since Greco-Roman time, architecture has gone through many transformations and changes, but through all of its changes the highest goal has always been the same: to create a space where people can live, think, and create. To simply make a building or a form has never been what architecture is about.

MA: If a student, not necessarily one involved with architecture, came to you and asked you for a recommendation of one book, what book would you suggest?

TA: Learning how to do architecture and learning how to live are the same thing. They involve the same principles and goals. Hmmm. Before I would recommend any book to a student, I would tell them to walk around and think first. Because if you read the book that I recommend, then you would be influenced by that book. But if you walk around and think, then you are influencing yourself. Learning to live is about walking around and thinking about ourselves and then influencing yourself through your thinking. After that you can read.

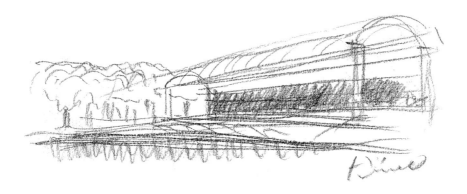

October 10, 1999

Michael Auping: How long have you known of Louis Kahn's work, and do you remember the first time you experienced a building by Kahn?

Tadao Ando: I have known of Louis Kahn's work for a long time. I have seen his buildings in Philadelphia; the Salk Institute in La Jolla, California; and the Indian Institute of Management in Ahmedabad.

MA: What do you think is his most important achievement?

TA: Without a doubt the Kimbell Art Museum.

MA: Why is that?

TA: First of all, it is a very elegant building, but more importantly it provides a sense of order that very few architects of the twentieth century have achieved. I think that architectural space creates consciousness, an awareness of a larger universal rhythm and balance. The quality of order that Kahn's buildings project, particularly the Kimbell, allows the viewer to sense this balance. We are then allowed to measure ourselves against it, to discover our own balance, to discover our own consciousness within this larger order. When I look at Kahn's work, I think of ancient Greek architecture. If you look at Kahn's sketches, you see the sense of order within Greek architecture. I remember his sketches of the Parthenon being very expressive but capturing something about the natural balance of the building. Even though the drawings are often very quickly done, you can feel it just in the way the marks are placed on the page. The basic thick marks that he makes have a strong rhythmic quality that gets translated into his buildings.

MA: Do you think your appreciation of Kahn's drawings has influenced the way you draw?

TA: Yes, probably, and Le Corbusier, as well, but I can't tell you exactly how. I'm sure there is something there that relates, but it is not something that has to do with style. It has to do with imparting a sense of this spatial order and its relationship to nature. Even though his sketches can be very colorful, the color does not overtake the sense of order. This sounds philosophically complicated, but it is very basic. It is at the very center of the art of architecture. It is this sense of order that I want to pursue in my work.

MA: In terms of your design for our building, are there any specific references to Kahn?

TA: I hope that it is this sense of order. The Kimbell has also made me think about the relationship between the horizontal and the vertical dimensions of architecture. For me, the horizontal aspect of architecture is very natural. It is connected to the land. However, the vertical is equally important. It is intentional. It corresponds to the existence and willfulness of man on earth. The vertical element in architecture corresponds to what type of mentality, what type of consciousness we have to this place. The challenge is to make the intentional seem natural. The Parthenon is an example of the use of verticality in its use of columns, but at the same time it is brought down to earth by horizontal lines. The Kimbell is another example of horizontality that is intentionally lifted gently up by the arching lines of the roof and ceiling. They are two different buildings that start at different points but meet at a place of balance.

MA: The cruciform shape that you have used in the churches you've designed, but also in other of your buildings that have large windows divided by cruciform mullions, would seem to be a good symbol for this relationship.

TA: Yes. It's an ancient symbol for balance, and in every strong building you can discover less obvious examples of this balance.

MA: Do you think this is a quality that Kahn's work shares with traditional Japanese architecture?

TA: Yes. It's a quality that all great architecture aspires to. Of course, I have been very influenced by traditional Japanese architecture. It has taught me, above all, that universal expressions aspire to simplicity. All art forms that mankind creates, whether they are old or new or made by different cultures, connect at very deep and universal levels. I think that all great architecture converges at a point of stillness. It is this stillness that human consciousness seeks.

MA: That is difficult to find in an advertising environment that creates and reinvents desire every few seconds. It seems to me we live in a very dense and complex world of postmodern images, yet your buildings seem radically simple, almost primitive in some ways. Do you aspire to a more ancient Japan than a contemporary, postmodern one?

TA: You could say that is true, but it is not a nostalgic or sentimental feeling. I have to live in this society like you do, so I must work through the chaos of this time the way every generation has to work through the chaos of their time. However, I do think that today cities are so much more complicated and dense that there is a real need to create spaces that suggest solitude and spiritual freedom. I think you do this through order and simplicity, not successive adornment. It should be a quality that people feel unconsciously, a feeling of awareness and contemplation. If you provide the essence of space and form, the individual will complete it with their imagination.

MA: The pavilions, the six pavilions of your original design for our building, are they a reflection of your admiration for the long pavilions that are part of Kahn's Kimbell? Are they a kind of homage to Kahn? I know you have said before that they make up the image of a swan, but they also seem very much related to the Kimbell design.

TA: I would not call it an homage to Kahn because these pavilions arose from my urge to create a relationship between the vertical and the horizontal, which is of course an eternal challenge. All architects must address it, including Kahn. In this case, I want to express the quality of horizontality, which connects it to this eleven-acre site. And the image of a swan on the water relates symbolically to this sense of horizontality. I would say, however, that the use of six pavilions in the original design relates generally to Kahn's use of six pavilions in the Kimbell. Of course, the forms are quite different. I have tried to embrace the horizontal openness of the site. I think the Kimbell is more compact. I would like to relate to Kahn's building subtly, without competing with it or mimicking it. Because the buildings are across from each other and in close proximity, I think it's important that the relationship be felt intuitively and not drastically.

MA: We have lost one of the pavilions for our building. So now our final design has five pavilions. I know that you have approved of this final design, but I have to ask, do you feel that losing the one pavilion has damaged the image that you originally had? Is it now a different building?

TA: It's the same building. What was the sixth pavilion is now a space of possibility. For me, the image is still the same—the image of a swan on a lake. It's like the image of a swan with part of one wing under the water. In the future at some time it will come out of the water. That part of the wing that is hidden under the water represents the possibility of the future for this image. It is the symbol of possibilities and of change in the future.

MA: Fort Worth provides a different landscape than you are accustomed to—more suburban, somewhere between the city and the country. Has that presented any problems?

TA: The challenge in a place like Texas—which has a vast natural landscape— is to ground this man-made structure to the openness of the land. On the one hand, to make something distinct and solid, but at the same time to integrate it into the land, to make it seem like a natural part of this land and not an artificial addition. The way to do that is through symbols, like the swan, and proportions. These are two powerful aspects of architecture.

MA: What would you say is the most basic proportional element in this building?

TA: As you know, the interior of the pavilions is organized on a series of twenty-four-foot squares. This is very important because I think the square is the most fundamental geometric form. I think of the famous image by da Vinci of the human form measured inside a square.[3] Our proportions and our being relate to the square like no other form. I want people to feel that sense of proportional fit when they are in this building. A square is a shape you cannot find in nature. It's a man-made shape. It was probably the first of the geometric forms that humans created. To me, however, it also relates very much to Texas. Although it is man-made and geometric, it also relates to natural space, to the openness of space. In Texas, the land or horizon is

3 Leonardo da Vinci's drawing *Proportions of the Human Figure (Vitruvian Man)*, 1490 shows the figure inside a square that is inside a circle, demonstrating the relationship between the two shapes.

very long but the sky is also very tall. It is like our vision articulates a square space, only in terms of proportion. It is a square you don't necessarily see. I hope the square shapes in this building will be apparent or felt but not necessarily seen. I would like to integrate these two types of universal space: that of nature and that which can be made by man.

To give you more examples of the use of the square, Le Corbusier once proposed an "Endless Museum," like an endless square. The shape of the wrapping cloth in Japanese culture is also a square, and it presents many possibilities for folding into different configurations. The square offers a certain sense of containment and freedom at the same time. Ancient writing, the letters used in ancient Hebrew or Islamic writings, are also in square frames.

MA: The square is a seemingly less manipulative or gestural form.

TA: Yes. It's a form of balance and for that reason more open in all directions. The square, although man-made, relates equally to the balance and openness of nature.

One of the other things that I am interested in is a corridor or colonnade space by Brunelleschi with a vaulted roof or cupola in the center, contained by a square and an X shape that help define the proportions. Once you are in a space like that you realize how a certain geometry can speak to you—to your intellect and your emotions. That is what we mean when we speak of a space as being eternal or universal. It is a kind of space that can function through many different times and cultures.

MA: If our building can achieve some of that quality, then the issue of using a Japanese architect in Texas will not seem odd at all.

TA: [laughing] No. In a sense, Texas is a perfect place to test these challenges because it is so open.

MA: I wanted to ask again about the ellipse. You mentioned before how it relates to Zen philosophy as a symbol of the eternal. Do you see the elliptical shape that you often employ as having the same eternal qualities as the square?

TA: Well, on one level, the circle and the ellipse are perfect shapes. However, the circle belongs to the sacred world, the world of the gods, and has eternal symbolic meaning. The ellipse belongs to the human world. It is a humanly expressive shape that represents a kind of movement. It represents liberal thinking. I think it can create a type of space that can motivate people to think and to move in space. It has a contemplative side but it functions in a more dynamic way.

MA: The moon's orbit is elliptical. So it is a shape that also has a natural element.

TA: Yes. It is a space that represents directional movement that is more specific than a circle. It is a space of action. It should suggest active thinking. For Fort Worth, I have placed an ellipse at the entrance of the gallery spaces. I felt that as you move through the orderliness of the twenty-four-foot square grid, which invokes calm and balance, that it would be good to come upon this ellipse that does not correspond to the grid.

MA: Do you think of this elliptical space as a kind of sculpture?

TA: I don't think it is a sculpture, but I think it is a sculptural space. Of course, sculpture and space are very connected. You can enter the elliptical space before going into the galleries. It is there as an exhibition space, but also to invoke thinking before people enter the galleries. It is a means of using a space to motivate a thinking action. It is there to stimulate thinking.

I also see the ellipse in a broader sense. I think the twenty-first century is an unknown space, a potentially very dynamic time, a time of new and liberal thinking, but also a time of some uncertainty. As a people, we need to be stimulated to think about the possibilities inherent in uncertainty, to be awakened to new possibilities. I want these ellipses to reflect this dynamic instability. I think the ellipse is a very good symbol of movement into the next millennium.

MA: Can we talk about the importance of the roof of a building? You have spent a lot of time designing the roof of this building, which may seem odd to some people because you really don't see the roof, except from the air. How do you imagine someone experiencing the roof of this building?

TA: Of course, every building needs a roof, but I also see the roof of this building as horizontal lines. This is important because it expresses an intention to integrate with the landscape and site. I would be happy not to have a roof, just well-proportioned rooms and walls for the art. But of course you have to have a roof for practical reasons. The roof is one of the more complicated aspects of a building, particularly a museum. It is like a special filter. For instance, you would like to have light come into the space to bring life to the rooms and the art in them. Many museums today are very tightly controlled in terms of using so much artificial light. I try to avoid that because it takes our experience further away from the natural. Natural light is very important because it brings the geometry of the space closer to nature. It's important to maintain a balance between the natural and the man-made. But as you know, too much natural light is a problem, so we have devised the special scrim to soften and spread the light. Also, the basic structure of the roof is concrete and this is important so that people can see the structural integrity of the building, the strength of this building. Like everything in architecture, it is a matter of balance between separating oneself from nature and inviting nature into the space.

Again, the Pantheon in Rome is a very good example for me. Not only are the proportions perfect and universal—putting a sphere inside a square building—but the quality of light coming from the center of the ceiling is eternal. The proportion between light and structure is perfectly balanced. There are very few spaces like it in the world. I believe that natural light is the soul of a space. It is like breath to a body. Human beings need light. It is extremely important to our being.

MA: You keep stressing the horizontal character of this building and its relationship to the natural condition of landscape, but for me one of the more moving aspects of this design is the quality of vertical lift I imagine feeling when looking up at this two-story structure of concrete clothed in glass. From a distance, I think one's sense of the building will be horizontal, but as you approach and enter it I think there will be a sense of verticality.

TA: Yes. There are various parts of this building that reach up to the sky. The Y-shaped structures that appear to hold up the roof overhangs are there to draw the eye upward.

MA: It almost looks like a human form with arms reaching upward, suspending the roof between the water and the sky.

TA: It can be seen like that. It is a vertical element that embraces the horizontal lines of the roof.

MA: It is a very grand building that I think will surprise people with its size—much larger than the Kimbell—and openness.

TA: It is larger, but I don't think it will seem overwhelming. I want to maintain the same intimacy and elegance as the Kimbell.

April 8, 2000

Michael Auping: I wanted to ask you more about qualities of light and how you use light to enhance your interiors, and perhaps the exteriors as well.

Tadao Ando: As I've mentioned to you in the past, the house that I grew up in is a very old Japanese rowhouse, a long rowhouse. One of the things that I remember most about it is that when you entered this house it was dark because the house was shut with walls on both sides, the south and the north. It had moments of light, but I have strong memories of this house because when you were in this house and the lights were not turned on, it was very dark, and within that darkness I felt that I was being enclosed. I felt secure, protected. I felt that the space of that house protected my body. This is a very fundamental feeling that I have about certain places and I remember first feeling it in that old, small Osaka house.

I visited a house this morning in Dallas, for instance, which is very beautiful, but it has no darkness. It is very clear and very bright. That is far different from my concept of a dwelling. I think a house serves the purpose of a dwelling both physically and spiritually, and it's my perception that darkness plays an important role in that.

MA: Ironically, most writers describe your buildings as being essentially about light.

TA: You are able to see the light because of the darkness. In my Osaka house you entered through a dark space and, as you walked through, various yet limited openings would allow light in. Because of the darkness you felt the strong presence of the light. If you look at a traditional Japanese house, you can see that it is difficult for light to enter the interior rooms directly because of the eaves and the transitional *engawa* space that surrounds the building. The interior is always illuminated by indirect light reflected from the *engawa* and the garden. So overall, it is relatively dark on the interior of the Japanese house. When you sit inside of a dark room and you look out at the garden that is naturally illuminated, you can begin to feel the fundamental

relationship between light and darkness, the reason they need each other to express themselves. I felt this in my childhood house. I appreciate it when people write about the light in my buildings, but I think it is also important to look at the shadows. They play an important role in my buildings. Shadows and darkness contribute to serenity and calmness. In my opinion, the darkness creates the opportunity to think and contemplate.

MA: In a Christian society, light is always privileged over darkness, darkness having an essentially evil connotation. Are you suggesting that darkness may even be more important to the contemplative, creative process?

TA: Yes, I think so. Of course, the balance of dark and light can shift depending on the context. But areas of darkness are critical, and I think they relate to deep metaphorical levels of creation. It seems to me that philosophers, poets, people who spend much of their life thinking about basic things, deep down in their mental state they have what I would call a scar. It is something deep within themselves or their past that provokes them to think of life in a different way. This scar gives them the will to fight or the strength to express themselves. Right now I am thinking about the architect Daniel Libeskind. He is Jewish and he seems to live with a scar of being Jewish, which is the scar of the difficult history of the Jews. That seems to be the imagery that drives his creativity. And there are important areas of darkness in his buildings.

MA: Do you think this is true of all successful architects?

TA: Many of the ones I can think of. We could talk about Louis Kahn and the achievement of a remarkable sense of architectural order, but you can see, even from photographs of him, that he is a fighter. His scar was recognized physically on his face as deep as his inside. Even his expressions indicated that he always had something on his mind, that he was trying to deal with something all the time, until the time he died. He was found dead in a public toilet at Penn Station in New York. His entire life seemed to be this battle with life, and the result of that battle was this incredible sense of order. The life of an architect is not meant to be a happy one. Once you feel content and happy, it probably means your search is finished, your incompleteness is gone or somehow forgotten.

We know that Kahn produced a number of truly important buildings, like the Kimbell and the Salk Institute. But I think the results of his innermost, primary nature are the works he did in Ahmedabad, India at the Institute of Management, and the National Capitol of Bangladesh in Dhaka. In those works, he pursued darkness to the extreme. The works that he did in the United States prior to that time can be regarded very highly in terms of suggesting what popular modern architecture could be, but the works he did in Asia express the very deep nature of his thinking. His evolution seemed to move from light to dark, using darkness as a more profound way of expressing himself.

MA: The next obvious question, of course, is how would you describe the scar that is expressed in your work?

TA: Well, generally speaking, Osaka—where I have spent most of my life—might be seen as on the periphery of Japanese culture. It is the last place someone would think of as cultural in the sense of fine modern art. The place where you are born and raised, and the time when you are born and spend most of your time are critical for people. By being born in 1941, when the Pacific War opened, and being raised in this peripheral place, I think I carry this unconscious scar or need to be deeply cultural. There were so many who suffered from poverty or destitution around me from 1945 to 1965. I understood as a young man that living is not an easy thing, that life can be severe. In my late teens, I wanted to affect culture, even if I was not born to it. I sometimes have this feeling that I am coming from someplace very low and am wanting to go beyond it. Perhaps Mr. Isozaki could understand what I am saying. He was born in Ohita, in Kyushu Island; he was also born in one of the peripheral places. If we can continue the metaphor of dark and light, I would say that we do not come from the bright light of a place like Tokyo, where you are in the center of the light of the cultural. We come from the country. We come from the shadows of the cultural scene. On the other hand, you have an architect like Mr. Maki, who was born and raised in a wealthy family in Tokyo. His work is lighter, you might say more dazzling, in appearance. He doesn't seem to carry any visible scar.

MA: Having known you for a few years now, and having visited Japan a number of times, it's a little difficult for me to see you in Tokyo, even though you now hold the Chair in Architecture at the University of Tokyo. You seem, I don't know . . . more ancient. I think of your Chikatsu Asuka Historical Museum outside Osaka. I think it is one of your greatest works, even more so than the highly acclaimed Church of the Light and Church on the Water. They are all unique buildings, but the Chikatsu Asuka Historical Museum literally took my breath away. Somehow I don't think an urbane, postmodern architect could design such a museum.

TA: Ancient! [laughs] I am not so old, but the area of Kyoto, Nara, and Osaka where I come from was once the center of ancient Japan. It has what is called a tomb culture, a tomb civilization. Of course, tombs exist all over the country, but there is a dense concentration of tombs around Nara and Osaka. When you are young, when you are growing up, your body responds to the environment, the physical environment as well as the spiritual environment. In my case, I was always aware of the great tombs surrounding us. These tombs have a very powerful presence—a place carved into nature that suggests a meditation on the past, the present, and the future. I think what you are suggesting, and it may be true, is that this tomb environment has affected me. Also, I value the instinctive synthesized wisdom and inborn abilities of native people and traditions. I prefer trying to solve difficult problems by referring back to native knowledge and solutions rather than consulting books of new theory.

MA: I'm just thinking out loud about what common threads run through all of your buildings and how far these characteristics will evolve. You began your career by building some very acclaimed private residences and then you became internationally known, it seems to me, for building churches. And most recently you have moved to larger, more public situations designing museums. Because all of your buildings have a protected and private quality about them, I'm wondering if you can imagine ever designing something as public and pedestrian as, say, an international airport? Isn't this mega-public project something that many architects strive for—the challenge of building something on that scale? How does one prepare oneself to make that leap from the private residence to the international airport?

TA: Well, my overriding goal as an architect has been to provide people with an architectural situation that nurtures the spirit. This is very important, of course, in the building of a house. The house protects the body, which holds the spirit. So the house must feel like a secure dwelling that comforts the body and the spirit. We have discussed this before. As the body must feel comfortable with the spirit inside it, the building must provide comfort, which means protection, but also places for reflection and meditation, not in a formal sense, but meditation in terms of one's thinking about their relation to the world. In terms of the museum, it is a matter of the ability of

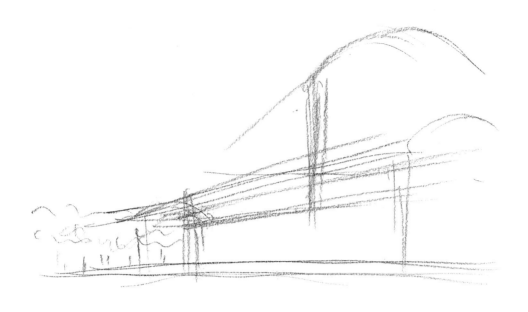

the architecture to enrich the relationship between the visitor and the art; ideally to enrich the spirit of the person to prepare them for the complex kinds of experiences they will have with the art. The church is a similar experience. All of these types of buildings require a basic condition that seems to be lacking in many buildings today: that is, a sense of security, protection.

MA: But many buildings protect us from the elements with four walls and a roof. That doesn't necessarily make them good buildings.

TA: This is true. I think the word *security* is more appropriate. To make someone feel secure enough with their environment that they would then feel comfortable enough to go within themselves. The relationship and balance between materiality and spirituality is an important one in architecture. All of the great architects have explored this issue. Architecture should offer people a place of possibilities. If you think about that goal and then you think about the context and goals of an airport, you can see the problem. An airport is a place of transition. The building must be designed to move people from one point to another. It's purely functional. There is no spiritual requirement. The point is to come and go as quickly as possible. There are, of course, some very beautiful and functional airports that have been designed in recent years. However, I do not have any interest in that kind of project. My goal is to try and provide spiritual fulfillment for people who use my buildings, and I don't think the goals of an airport and my goals would work well together.

MA: If it's all right, I'd like to return to a discussion of our Fort Worth building. We now have the foundation of the building nearly complete. The building will begin to come out of the ground soon. What is occupying your thinking right now in regard to our building? What are you most concerned about at this stage of the project?

TA: As you know, when the foundation of any building starts to become visible, you see the backbone, and it is very exciting to see this basic form taking shape. At the same time, you can't help but wonder exactly what the eventual form will be, from backbone to outer skin. Even if you have made hundreds, maybe thousands, of drawings, you can't know exactly what it will look like until it is built. So you watch and wonder and have anxiety about whether it will grow into a good building or a bad building. This is not something we talk about—you may feel some anxiety, too—but we keep it to ourselves. It is this anxious drama that I have been dealing with lately. Certainly we have designed this building very carefully with so much thought that we think we know what it will look like, but you really don't know until it starts to come out of the ground. Also, this is a large structure occupying a fairly vast site. The transformation from drawings to actual building will be dramatic. So it is exciting but also a little frightening.

MA: On Thursday, we went down into the basement to see some of the big concrete walls. You noticed some problems with coloration and surface. I know these basement walls will not be seen by the public, but it won't be long before we begin pouring walls that will be prominent features of the building, and you have always been very precise about the quality of your concrete. What are your primary concerns right now in terms of the concrete for our building and the feeling you would like the concrete to impart?

TA: Well, the mock-ups that we did last year on the site are generally very good, but mock-ups are always good. People pay attention when they are making mock-ups. It's keeping that attention on building the actual walls that is important. That is my main concern right now.

MA: What is the feeling or image you are striving for in these walls? Is it fair to ask how the technical aspect of pouring these walls will communicate your vision?

TA: Well, when Mies van der Rohe built his German Pavilion in Barcelona, he used stones as building material in a perfect, subtle manner. He was a son of a stone layer and he learned to appreciate the qualities of stones better than many other architects I can think of. Of course, when you talk about materials there are degrees of understanding. For example, most people understand that wood has grains and we have to respect the qualities of those grains. However, not many people understand that stone also has a grain that has to be respected and used carefully in order to bring out the life within that stone. I think Mies van der Rohe could see the life within the stone and he could bring it out when he used it in his buildings. The German Pavilion in Barcelona reflects his appreciation of glass as a universal material and the life within stones. He created a space that is imbued with the life of these materials. It is not just the shape of a building, but the spirit of the materials that creates the space. Having said this, I have some doubts that the German Pavilion we see today is the same one that existed in 1929 when he built it. I'm not sure that the same sensitivity to material has been passed on to those who have cared for the building over the years.

MA: How would you describe the spirit or soul of concrete?

TA: I tend to think of concrete as being very hard and sharp. I like the sharp edges and planes that can be made with concrete. When they come into contact with nature they are like a powerful foil. The precise order in contrast to nature can make both elements more dynamic. However, over the years of using this material, I have come to see different qualities of concrete. Depending on the space I am trying to construct, I may see it as just the opposite: softer and less severe. Even though in general, I appreciate the hardness, strength, and geometric sharpness of concrete, this may not work for every kind of space and the perception of that quality can be changed with the use of natural light. No material functions exclusively on its own. It is always affected by the context of other materials and natural conditions.

MA: In America, it seems very easy to take concrete for granted. Our sidewalks and freeways are made of it. We live in an essentially concrete landscape. It all looks alike.

TA: Yes. It appears to be a very common material that is available every-where, and because it is generally used in only one way we think of it as being very one-dimensional. However, concrete possesses many variables. Every concrete mix and pour has a different character. It is not like steel or glass, which has a more consistent nature. Concrete can vary greatly. Concrete has a depth of expression that changes with every use. Le Corbusier used concrete as if it were clay. He used its plastic quality almost as if he were sculpting. Louis Kahn used concrete as if it were hard steel. The same mater-ial; two very different effects. In Kahn's case, however, you can see that the same use of concrete can look very different depending on context. I think the best example of this is the Salk Institute in La Jolla. The quality of the concrete at the Salk Institute and the Kimbell is similar, but the locations are different and give different meanings to the surface. The Salk is so embed-ded in the natural—the stone coastline and the water—that it seems to bring the man-made quality of the concrete alive in a more pronounced way.

MA: I have to ask about the story that many American writers cite in regard to your intense respect for the pouring of concrete. It's said that you once punched a worker who casually threw a cigarette butt into a form as concrete was being poured into it. Is this true, or a myth built around your boxing background?

TA: I don't recall this particular case in terms of a cigarette butt being thrown into the mix, but I can't deny that similar situations have taken place. It is not so much the case now, but twenty years ago these types of incidents took place on a daily basis. I am very concerned that workers take responsibility for their craft. Even an average building will last fifty years and we all must live with it over that time. So it is important to pay attention to what you are making.

MA: Visiting the site yesterday, seeing the foundation, do you have any new thoughts about how we will perceive this building when we first see it?

TA: This building will be about horizontality. It is very important for this building. I think it is its most unique quality. We can see the horizontal in many things, but this is a very intentional horizontality and that is not typical. Because the site is vast, we need to embrace that space. It isn't important to fill the space but to activate it—to make one aware of the nature of that space.

   I also think the large water surface around the museum will play an important role in our perception of this building. I think what architects always hope they can do is create both a reality and a fiction simultaneously. For this museum, the verticality of the building as it rises from the ground up will have a fictional element. Normally the building would stand on the ground and rise up. In this case, however, it will appear to stand on this surface of water. It will appear slightly to float on this surface, I think, and at the same time, it will project its fictional image onto the surface of the water. As people experience this combination of reality and fiction, I hope the space of this structure will seem to expand. It will have a resonance that is bigger than the physical structure. I am very excited about the possibility of experiencing the spatial relationship between the real and the fictional.

MA: It's an interesting and anxious time for all of us. It's probably good to have some curiosities and doubts. The good thing is that Fort Worth has just survived a tornado, and the young tree we planted at the ground-breaking ceremony last year as a gesture of good luck also made it through the tornado.

TA: This is a good omen.

September 18, 2000

Michael Auping: Now that the walls are coming out of the ground the build-ing is looking much larger in relation to the site than I thought. Given the fact that we have eleven acres, it seems almost aggressive. It's very surprising to me. Is that an illusion?

Tadao Ando: Partially, yes. When the walls first come out of the ground they have a very powerful presence. They are made of the earth and they appear to grow out of it. Even I, who have seen this happen many times, am always inspired by the raw presence of the concrete. We talk so much about the surface of the concrete, which of course is important here, but this building is not just about surface. There is the sheer power of the wall. Depending on how they are placed in relation to the site, they can have an amazing presence. They announce the building as a place. And when you can witness them actually come out of the ground, as you have, it gives a very strong impression. That's particularly the case when you see a wall come out of the ground without any openings. It's a monolithic statement.

MA: Like an ancient marker.

TA: Yes. That is part of the language of architecture, to announce itself, to mark a place. It must seem natural to that place, not just placed on a piece of land. But it is still early. You have been used to looking at flat floor plans and now you measure your body against the actual structure and it's very different. The first experience is of the walls surging out of the ground with a certain aggression, but as you experience it over time, they will appear to settle into the site. In proportion to the site the building is really not that big, although it may seem so at times, depending on where you are stand-ing. If you look at the ground coverage of the building in relation to the whole site, the percentage of building is about twenty percent. What you are seeing now is the first life of a wall—its presence in the outside world—how it stands in the world and announces its presence. However, every wall has two lives. When the building begins to create an interior space, then the second life exists on the interior of the concrete wall. On the inside, the wall does not reflect nature but the idea of shelter, and in the case of a museum, it is a particular type of shelter that produces a space that is serene

安藤忠雄建築研究所
〒531　大阪市北区豊崎2丁目5-23　PHONE.06(375)1148

and contemplative. The surface of concrete also has many faces. On the inside, with a roof and skylights, the surface will be softer and warmer and the light will change over the course of a day. At any given time of day that wall will never look exactly the same. It can reflect the moods of light.

MA: So you don't feel this Fort Worth building has an aggressive aspect, regardless of the power of these concrete walls.

TA: It's a good question, and perhaps there are some aspects of the form that could be described as aggressive, though that seems too strong a term. It may have its assertive qualities, but something can be assertive in a quiet way. Because of the horizontality of this design, I think it will project a quietness in its character. It is very tied to the land and nestled into the site. I can see that you are thinking of it as very powerful on the outside and very subtle on the inside. I know you have written about the intimacy you see in these spaces. Actually, I see it almost in reverse. When you first come upon this building I think that it will appear very subtle and serene. When you get on the inside, however, and you see the concrete, this natural, rock-like material, you will begin to feel the real power of the building. Much of the power of this building will be on the inside.

MA: It seems to me that the concept of this design is intrinsically tied to the idea of closing the gap, as it were, between nature and culture, not just in the Japanese sense, but in a nineteenth-century American sense. Many of our great museums built at the turn of the century were built in parks and next to lakes. You often see zoos built in these parks as well. I'm thinking of Olmsted's parks and the museums built within them: the Metropolitan Museum of Art, the Albright-Knox Art Gallery, etc. So when a family went to the museum they weren't in fact just going to a museum, but going to a complex in which art and nature were brought together.

TA: Yes. I understand what you are saying and I think this is important and a concept that is getting lost. I, of course, approach it from a Japanese point of view but as you say it is essentially the same philosophy. The *engawa* that is designed for this building, that space between the concrete and the exterior glass, is very symbolic of this philosophy and I think it will work to bring nature and art together in a way that is very unique. Because the art will be on the most inside spaces, I don't think it will have to compete with nature, but you will feel the presence of nature everywhere in this building.

MA: We have talked before about your interest in designing buildings based on your response to a site, and you have focused on the water element and the swan symbolism of the shape. But could you talk a little more specifically about the shape and topography of this site—perhaps in relation to the sun—and what it implies in regard to your design?

TA: Well, as I have said many times before, the surrounding context of any site is very important, and in this case the most prominent feature of the site is not the topography but the proximity of the Kimbell. The other thing is that both the Kimbell and the Modern have relatively vast pieces of land that ask to be filled or energized. And finally, the Modern's site is bordered on two sides by very busy streets that are visually aggressive and create noise. So these are the three main aspects of the site. I have tried to create a design that addresses all three.

First of all I have tried to create a design that has a sympathetic dialogue with the Kimbell. As I have said so many times, I greatly respect Louis Kahn's work and did so long before I was hired for this project. So this project has been a way to offer Mr. Kahn my gratitude and respect. The pavilions for the Modern are partly inspired by the pavilions at the Kimbell. They are classical rectangular units of space and form. Our roof is approximately the same height as the Kimbell's. This was not my opportunity to dominate, but to create a dialogue between generations. There are, of course, many differences. Our roof is flat in relation to the vaulted roof of the Kimbell pavilions. Since our entrances do not face each other, however, we can create our own space. For the Modern, the pond will be a central element, which the galleries and the restaurant and the lobby entrance face. I have tried to protect the site, creating an arbor, on all sides—shielded from the streets by landscaping on one side and the pavilions on the other. The effect is that of an arbor.

MA: It's a little like the ancient castles in Kyoto, in which a central sacred space is protected by layers of nature and architecture.

TA: Yes. And the glass walls create an *engawa*. It is a very contemporary building, but there is no question that it retains this Japanese aspect. As we have talked about before, the vastness of the site is addressed by the horizontal character of the pavilions.

MA: Could we return to this idea of architecture and fiction that you brought up before? Are we talking about aspects of illusion? There is a difference between fiction and illusion. An illusion is a kind of deceit; a fiction is a story.

TA: Well, I'm thinking of fiction and the difference between that and function. For most buildings, there is a function and a fiction. In this case, the reality is that it is a museum that must have practical functions: a restaurant, an auditorium, bathrooms, etc. However, if you want to call this architecture in a historical sense, then you have to apply a fiction. You can look at any city and see that many of the buildings have no fiction. They are purely functional. They don't give people anything to think or dream about. They exist without inspiring people. The difference between a building and architecture is fiction. The Kimbell, for example, is a very ordered fiction. It's very defined, and that ordered definition can inspire us in a very subtle way.

So for our museum of contemporary art in Fort Worth, the beginning of the fiction is the wall and that is followed by a ceiling and light coming down the wall. This is the beginning of the fiction, and you could try to fix that fiction in place, but I would like it to be a changing fiction. As you walk through this museum, the spaces will change in size and sometimes in shape and the light will change. As you go through the building, the scenes will change, the mood will change, the fiction will change. If they are subtle enough then you will not think of it as fiction or a story, you will just live it as reality.

MA: What you describe is very similar to how I think about sculpture. Some would say that the only difference between sculpture and architecture is that one has windows. How would you describe the relationship or the differences between the two?

TA: Well, I think when you talk about the role of fiction and illusion in architecture there is really no border between sculpture and architecture. They can be the same. There is no need to draw a line. However, architecture in all its aspects relates to people in a different way than sculpture. Architecture must carry practical functions, and people relate to it in relation to how they use it. It is usually the fictional that allows architecture and sculpture to have a dialogue. We need to keep in mind, however, that there are different fictions. The Miró that is outside the Kimbell Art Museum now seems not a good marriage, because that architecture and that sculpture belong to different fictions.

MA: But doesn't a museum have to accommodate many fictions? It has to be generous enough to . . .

TA: Yes. That's very true. It may be that the Miró is not sited properly. In cases like that it is a collision of fictions. So the site, the building, and the art all have to be considered in making these fictions work together. That will be your job and I sense that you can do it very well. So with architecture the fiction does not stop when the building is built. It continues. In a museum, the curator is the one who extends the fiction, or he can stop a fiction from happening. So the eventual fiction of architecture depends on how the building is used. The curator is responsible for the art, but also in many ways for the building as well.

MA: When curators and architects or architects and artists disagree, it seems to me it is not a matter of different style, but something deeper, like sensibility, for lack of a better word. It's something everyone has and, as we've talked about, comes from early experiences. I have often wanted to ask you, what were some of your earliest art experiences? When did you first become aware of art and the fiction of art? Who are some of the artists you've admired?

TA: Well first of all, sensibility is a deep aspect of architecture, and there are many ways that you develop this sensibility and learn architecture at the same time. One way, for example, of learning how to make architecture is to go to school. This is the conventional way. You study what we might call the printed materials and you learn how to make buildings according to the information in these books. You feed your mind with information and then try to sort out that information. However, I did it in a different way. I did it through my body. I worked around craftsmen and builders, who I thought of as artists. So the basis of my relationship with architecture is physical and my perception of architecture is related to this physicality. The physical presence of architecture is the foundation of my sensibility. This is more important for me than anything else. This is my sense of reality, which I got at a very early stage. So many very brilliant people go to the best universities and study art and philosophy before they ever learn to build anything. Their process is the reverse of mine. In the end, however, we all come to the reality of what makes architecture and not just a building.

My understanding of art and philosophy came much later and is important to me, but remains secondary to this sense of the physical. When I was perhaps a teenager, there was a group of artists who you probably know of—the Gutai. I learned from them, and I felt that I related to them because they were involved in how art comes from the body. They were also very clear about the physical aspect of art. In America, you had Jackson Pollock and he was also involved in a perception of the body and its relation to space. So I approached architecture from two physical sides: the physical presence of a form and the perception of the body in space, in which the Gutai were part of my learning.

So the body is the center of my architecture rather than the book, which I think is different than the orientation of many architects today. For example, Peter Eisenman reads Derrida and then interposes that to the making of architecture, which has interesting results. I always read later, when I have time to read.

MA: I know we have touched on this before, and I don't want to mythologize your interesting past, but could we say that your time as a boxer relates to this need for the physical? Sometimes when I am standing near one of your large concrete walls emerging from the ground, I imagine the thrust of a boxer's arm, a fist firing out from the body.

TA: [laughter] I don't know. For me, the relation between the boxing and architecture has to do with a maintaining of anxiety and tension, and using that as a creative force. For example, when you are a boxer, you prepare for long periods for rounds that will last only three minutes. The anxiety and tension of thinking about what to expect and how to move and respond in relation to the moves of your opponent will begin at least a week before the match. Boxing is a little more intense than most sports, where you can be aware of the excitement of competition, and you are aware of your training and how to use it. In boxing you are operating on pure instinct. In that sense, it's not sport. It's a fight, a very basic, primitive condition. For the week before, however, it is all thinking; and then for the match, it's only physical.

MA: So in terms of our building, where are we? A week before the match?

TA: [laughter] No. We are almost twelve months into construction. We are physical. So we are beginning to operate on instinct. I think we are in the ring. [laughter]

MA: At least we are shedding some anxiety and getting our hands dirty. Waiting for a building that has never before existed and requires the labors of literally many hundreds of people is very nerve-racking. You are used to it. I'm not.

TA: No. It's always this way until it is finished. Architecture is a very long match, much longer than three minutes. And this tension is important. Many times architects begin to get accepted, then become famous, and they lose this tension. As in sports, they may decide to do it just for the fun of it, or just because people expect them to. At that point, they are no longer in the heart of their profession.

MA: There is a question that I think needs to be asked of any architect who builds a museum, and that is should the architecture be a kind of neutral background or stage, as it were, so the art can be the main actor? When you build a private home, you are building it for one family, one vision. When you build a museum, you are designing it for many different visions.

TA: It's a matter of how an architect approaches his field. A museum is, of course, a place where you exhibit art, and to exhibit something you need a background for the thing to express itself. This has given rise to the idea of the museum as the perfectly neutral space, the white room where you could put almost anything inside and it appears beautiful. That philosophy is not that different than showing merchandise. You have a piece of clothing you want to sell and so you want it to stand out in the most exaggerated way. So you make the perfect empty space and you shine light on it and it exists as a kind of trophy. Many museums deal with their art this way and many architects create spaces this way. And that's fine, but it is not the only way to respect art. For example, the Kimbell space may not have that idea of pure neutrality but art can be very beautiful there. It is not a perfectly contained white room. It has variables: curves and the addition of natural, changing light. However, some art looks very beautiful there.

MA: Absolutely. I am not one of those people who feel that museums should be pristine white and ultimately flexible. Interesting spaces, if they are reasonably proportioned, allow the curator and the artist to make an installation that is special in that place. If you really believe in the power of art, you know that it can withstand and project in many different kinds of spaces. Art shouldn't be treated like something that is so frail that it requires the clinical character of an operating room. I like to think that there is a difference between an art museum and a Prada showroom.

TA: Of course, but many museums today do approach that condition. I think that Kahn looked at art as constituting different lives and you want to treat them as living things and not as merchandise. You want to be able to help sustain the life of each work by giving it a living condition, a sense of spatial energy that can include nature and natural light, things that are not always perfectly controllable. A museum is not simply a display case, but a space that brings life to what is inside it. At the same time, we understand that too many variables can distract from the art. So it is always a balance.

MA: How does a building like the Guggenheim in Bilbao fit into this discussion? Gehry's design is so dynamic that when I went there and people asked me what show I saw, it took me a while to remember because all I could think about was the form of the building.

TA: It is a very interesting building and I think that it is basically a work of sculpture. You could say that it is ninety percent sculpture and ten percent architecture.

MA: Maybe that is the kind of image modern urban museums require today to compete in our hyper-visual environment.

TA: That may be true, but that is not my way. I don't want to compete in that way. I think there are other avenues for dealing with urban problems and urban spaces.

May 16, 2001

Michael Auping:You have just been to the construction site. What did you see, or more specifically, what did you like and what, if any, problems did you find?

Tadao Ando: Well, we are more than halfway through and we have to pay very careful attention now. There are always concerns along the way in making sure that the form does not diverge from the original concept and meaning of the vision. But details become very important. The structure is almost a completed building from the outside. Once it is completely enclosed, we start interior finishes and we have to watch that very carefully. The interior of this building is its soul. You pay as much attention as you can to the pouring of the concrete, but if you don't pay the same attention to the granite and wood floors, it will not complete the vision. If you go to a Japanese temple, you see that nothing is disregarded. You could say that every material, every joint, is sacred.

MA: We have to compete with complacency.

TA: In boxing, once you let your guard down, it's over.

MA: We tore one wall down recently because the coloration was not as good as we would like—splotchy and not very uniform. I know you were ambivalent about tearing it down, thinking that it might dry and the coloration even out. I don't think any of us wanted to tear it down, but because it was one of the spaces in the museum where I would be hanging art on concrete, it seemed important that the wall be as perfect as possible. In retrospect, what are your thoughts on this?

TA: Well, to discuss an individual wall is not always productive because a wall is part of a larger whole. You really never see just one wall. You see an overall room or structure. I was hoping that we could wait and see the overall struc-ture, all of the walls, before we made a decision to tear it down. I would like

to have seen the overall finish of the walls before making a decision. However, looking now at the recast of that wall, I think the result is very good. In the end, I think we did the right thing.

MA: I think—hope—that we are both very happy with the size and proportion of the galleries. One thing that does strike me is how the walls throughout the museum have different personalities, as it were. In some buildings, you always feel you are looking at the same wall, no matter what room you are in.

TA: A wall is like an object that questions. When you look at a wall, there is space in front of it and space behind it. A wall relates two spaces. It can question their relationship or make you think about their relationship. There is always the question, for instance, of what is behind a wall. A wall should encourage people to think.

MA: What would you say are the physical characteristics of a good wall and why are there so many bad walls in buildings?

TA: A good wall, as you call it, is a matter of its physical relationship to people and the way it can create space around us, a system of spatial relationships. It is very basic, but something that people, including architects, often forget. It's very good to think about the wall. If you look at one wall in front of you, you can perceive it as an object. If you see it from the side, you understand that it divides space. If it then connects with another wall, you begin to see it as a container of space. At that point, the wall functions as a shelter, protection, a sense of security from the elements. This is the most primitive function of a wall, but it is a part of any important architecture. Creating spaces that inspire a sense of well-being is the main goal of building walls. To define the physical characteristics is a challenge. A wall must assert its presence in terms of its form and materiality, to make you understand that it has its own power or presence, but it must do so in a way that inspires and does not force or intimidate.

MA: Louis Kahn said that a wall is created when you put two bricks together.

TA: It is that basic. Then it becomes a matter of placement and proximity. It's important to be forceful without being intimidating or overly elaborate.

MA: Do you see concrete as a material that can be strong but gentle at the same time?

TA: Absolutely. It is natural and of the earth, yet it is a modern invention that can be manipulated—hopefully not over-manipulated. Because concrete can take almost any form, there can be a tendency to create forms that are too elaborate. When this happens we lose the presence of the material itself, and it becomes just manipulated design. You lose a sense of the weight and surface of the material, which is partly what inspires a sense of protection.

There is also the light. A wall catches light. That is another function of the wall. If you don't have a wall, the presence of light is not felt.

MA: What are some of the differences you see between an outside wall and an inside wall? In our building, we have concrete walls on the inside and the outside.

TA: That is a good point. It is the same wall, but it relates to different feelings and contexts. From the inside, we see the wall as an enclosure, as I talked about earlier. It forms space and protects us. An outside wall relates to an exterior context, to the city, or a surrounding landscape. From the outside, the wall creates form, and that form defines itself in relation to its surroundings. Its presence can set off its surroundings if the context is nature, or defend itself from them if it is an urban situation. The wall is the most basic tool of architecture.

MA: Like a piece of site-specific sculpture.

TA: Yes, but with other requirements that have to do with housing, protection, function. For a building to be successful, the inside and the outside must relate closely. The functional aspects of the spaces must have a dialogue through their form with the outside environment.

MA: Do you begin by thinking about walls from the outside in or the inside out?

TA: It changes with each project. However, it is important to begin with the site and establish what type of form the site can accommodate, and then create a form in which the spaces function for the client. In that sense, you begin from the outside in, but you have to move in both directions at the same time to create the dialogue between the inside and the outside. In this Fort Worth building, we have glass walls on the outside and concrete walls on the inside, which I think will make people think about different ways of opening and enclosing space.

MA: In regard to the Fort Worth building, could we talk specifically about the hanging metal panels that cover the façade? We will all be seeing those mock-ups tomorrow. Do you imagine these metal panels as a kind of wall, and can you describe for me the effect you hope they will have? They are the first thing a visitor will see when they enter the museum.

TA: The metal panels are a system similar to the glass curtain walls. The glass and the metal perform a similar function in that they both hang outside a concrete interior. They wrap around a concrete form. The interior concrete wall is the wall that protects you. The glass and metal panels are a transition to the outside. The glass and the metal can be considered walls, but they are different types of walls than the concrete. They function very differently.

MA: I understand the concept of a transitional wall—like an *engawa*, a space between the inside and the outside—when it comes to the glass. You can see through glass, but you can't see through metal.

TA: The surface of the metal has a number of functions. It is both soft and hard, and will absorb and reflect. What I want to achieve is a sense of lightness, like a curtain. This curtain is a way of softening the exterior so that the building will have a more graceful presence in the surrounding landscape of this park and pond. The hanging metal and the hanging glass are meant to be a counterpoint to the gravity and weight of the interior concrete. Even though you cannot see through it, the lightness of the metal panels will be intuitively understood as being of the same system as the glass, a more gentle outer layer. So, as we have talked about before, the concrete walls are the protective core of the structure, the glass and metal are the softer outer shell, and the space in between is the *engawa*. I see the metal like a *shoji* screen. Relative to the gravity of the concrete, it is like a paper screen—something that creates a space but is very light. The Western concept of a wall is always something very strong, powerful, and thick. In the East, we have a number of ways of approaching the concept of a wall.

MA: I had a chance some months ago to go visit La Tourette, the Dominican monastery designed by Le Corbusier. I was surprised that it was dominantly concrete. Of course I thought of your work and the challenge of making a space of light and spirit out of a material that is so heavy. I know that you named your beloved dog Le Corbusier and that you admire Le Corbusier. I'm sure you've seen La Tourette. What are your thoughts about it and this idea of making a spiritual space out of concrete?

TA: This is a long story that I will try to keep short. Le Corbusier started in the 1920s with what we call the "white period," in which he made buildings and villas in white that appeared very abstract. At that time, he wanted to convey his ideals, his new image of architecture as something pure, strongly abstract, and universal. It was the image of that time to free architecture restricted by the weight of the past and he was very much a part of that time. Later, however, he went on to work with brick and concrete, and by that point I think he felt free enough to return to himself as a human being and ask himself what does he need to create; what kind of space does he personally need? That became La Tourette and some other buildings of that period. La Tourette is a very personal artistic work. It's almost like a sculpture of light, a place to receive light. And he wanted people to be able to live in a place that could receive light for the sake of the spirit and the mind. In La Tourette he transcended the age of modernism or his generation to make something very personal.

MA: The rectory is a fabulous space—long, narrow, high-ceilinged, and filled with light. The pavilions of our new museum, even the lobby—which we haven't talked much about—seem to aspire to a similar feeling or sensibility. Would you agree with that?

TA: Well, I want the lobby to be very receptive to light, but I see it as even more open as a space. When you walk into the lobby of the Fort Worth building, you will immediately see through the back wall of glass to the water beyond. I want the lobby to be perceived as an integrated part of the water—that it is all one long space, as if you are outside but protected.

MA: That is really very different from La Tourette.

TA: It is, in the sense that La Tourette is very much about containment with light penetrating the containment. Also, at La Tourette the gravity, the sense of weight, is very strong. Here I'm trying to balance the weight and gravity of the concrete with the lightness of the glass.

MA: We seem to be in a moment when architects are rock stars, where an architect goes to a city and is commissioned to build an iconic entertainment center, and then people come to pay reverence to the icon. I don't want to ask you whether you like this or don't like it, but why do you think this has occurred?

TA: There are many factors involved in the answer to that question. First of all, there is the media. This is a time of the media. Marshall McLuhan was right. Now we can appreciate the true meaning of the phrase "The medium is the message." Architecture is now carried by all media. If Frank Gehry builds a museum in Bilbao, it will be featured in every media. Everyone will know about it. The other part of the answer to that question is that people need stimulation. They want to have experiences and emotions. They want to be surprised. With the ease of travel today, everyone can go, and all these things—media, a need for new stimulations, and the ability to travel—come together to make architecture more than simply a place to house people or things.

MA: So seeing architecture has become a kind of popular adventure tour?

TA: Yes, in a way. Architecture plays a different role in a postmodern world.

MA: For me, the term *postmodernism* always seems to confuse things, if for no other reason than so few people seem to know what it is. Maybe we could talk about that. Postmodernism, it seems to me, is about deconstruction and collage—either tearing forms apart or collaging historical forms together. What do you see as the differences between modernism and postmodernism, and how does your work and philosophy relate to either term?

TA: Well, many historians believe that modernism began with the Industrial Revolution, when common working people began to have ideals, began to feel that they had certain rights, and that class structure was collapsing. The Industrial Revolution brought about a certain sense of comfort to many levels of society, a lifestyle that at one time only belonged to upper classes. These ideals that began with the Industrial Revolution continued for the most part until about 1960. At that point, many people began to consider the possibility that those ideals were either completed or no longer relevant. Postmodernism did not begin in the field of architecture. It was a philosophical movement fueled by many French thinkers. It was a broad effort to try to reinvigorate cultural investigations in the twentieth century—something that was not modernism but had the same sense of idealistic rigor. When you only look at architecture in relation to the postmodern movement, you see a lot of eclecticism, an overlaying of many iconic, historical elements. For me, that has never been a good solution to the problem of how to establish new forms of thinking. One of the problems has been that when this postmodern sensibility in architecture came into contact with commercialism it ceased being a viable expression and became a commodity. Everything became a matter of surface imagery, a world of interchangeable surfaces, depending on the fashion of the moment. I work with only a few materials in the context of natural elements. So on the one hand, I wouldn't fit into this initial idea of postmodernism. Before the 1960s and 1970s, there had never been a building with exposed concrete on the inside and the outside, a purely concrete structure. For me, this embrace of a material purity relates to a broader idea of postmodernism, particularly the French philosophers who were inquiring about the presence of things—not just the surface of things, but the presence of a material and space. This is the way to create a new world, from the inside to the outside, creating a space from one material, like concrete. It is not just about the meaning of a surface. In a way, I want the surface to disappear and become a space, a space that stimulates thinking. If the surface does not speak too loud, then people will begin to think about themselves. They bring the meaning to the space.

April 5, 2002

Michael Auping: Many people who have come to see the Fort Worth museum in the last few weeks seem to be surprised at what they call its "monumentality." It seems a little strange in that it is not, relatively speaking, that big. Do you see it as monumental, and if you do or do not, how do you define "monumental"?

Tadao Ando: I think it is very difficult to speak about "monumentality" in terms of architectural thought. First of all, I would say that the Fort Worth building is at a critical point in its relation to the landscape. The building has been set into the topography in a very specific way, using the natural grading of the site to create a space where architecture and landscape come together. Although as architects we often talk about doing this, in reality it is never easy to do, to allow nature to play an important role.

MA: Unless you have the inland Sea of Japan as your backdrop. A number of your buildings create a dialogue with that ocean, which is a very powerful, natural image.

TA: Yes. Architects always talk about the buildings, but what many people remember about a building is the scenery in which it is placed, how you see the structure relating to nature. This has always been very important in my buildings and to the history of Japanese architecture. In the case of Texas, which is very broad and flat, we have had to help create a special situation. As you know, we have saved many trees on the Fort Worth site, but we also have had to add some. This was partly for protection from the surrounding streets and intersections, but also a part of the concept of creating an arbor for art. So as you know, we are at a critical point now, adding trees to complete this concept. How this building relates to the landscape that existed and that we are creating is very important. The grass and trees affect the light, and the clustering of trees affects certain viewing angles. It's all part of a whole, and it is this whole, not the building as an isolated structure, that could be seen as monumental.

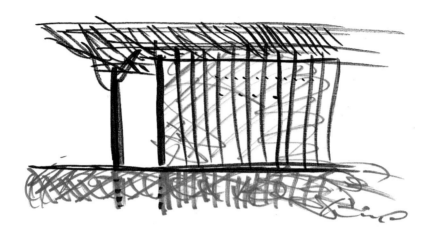

MA: So you don't think of the building as monumental.

TA: When you visit Ronchamp Church by Le Corbusier, you couldn't say that it is a big building, but you could say that it has characteristics of the monumental. The way it is situated on the landscape and the way you approach it allows a sense of anticipation. It's not its size but the way it rises out of the landscape as the viewer approaches that gives you the sense that you have arrived at a place of importance. Context and approach are very important. The same is true on an interior. At Ronchamp, again, there is a sense of the grandness of the space, the way the ceilings rise in the right places at the right height. That has characteristics of the monumental. I hope that Fort Worth can have some of these characteristics. If it does, then when visitors leave they will take away the idea of this type of monumental space in their memory. That type of space gives people a sense of their own importance, of their own dignity.

MA: Is this what you had in mind in designing the new Armani runway in Milan? I've been curious about the fact that the architect of churches and museums would suddenly design a fashion runway. It seems to me such a different world.

TA: Well, I don't think I am an architect solely devoted to designing churches and museums. I will be happy to accept the challenge of any type of project that has caught my interest. In regard to churches and museums, those worlds seem to be coming closer together, but that is a longer discussion. From my point of view the space for Armani should have the same meaning, that is to give a sense of dignity to the human presence in that space, whether it is a fashion show or something else. In a museum, the main subject is the relationship between the artwork, the people, and the space. In contemporary society, people increasingly understand that they are the subject. We talk about how we see things, how the world revolves around us. Of course, this is important because if people don't feel their own presence, their own importance, they won't begin to open up to the other things around them. So the first thing is giving people a sense of their individual dignity. As architects we have to be conscious of this self-awareness. I hope that when people enter that space they feel as important as the models. But you also have to take people out of themselves to the larger experience. The Armani building was not designed just as a place for models to present clothing and walk in front of the audiences. It is not just a space of display.

In that sense, it's the same as a museum. Why did Mr. Armani choose me as an architect for this theater? We know that he has so many architects and designers around him who are willing to work for him. I would like to think Mr. Armani expected me to create something that presents a sense of permanence or eternity in the transitory world of fashion. In consultation with Mr. Armani, what we have tried to do is create a broader social space, a theater, a place for different types of events—in other words, a place for people to gather. Hopefully, it's not just a runway or boutique but a kind of living theater.

MA: Let me ask you about your most recent commission, the Pinault project, which I think is your most ambitious undertaking to date. It's very interesting to me because I think the Fort Worth building will be evaluated initially on its own merits and its relationship to your previous buildings; but eventually it will also be evaluated on its relationship to what comes after. I'll be curious to see, and I'd like your thoughts on this, if the Fort Worth building led to something or was the culmination of a phase.

TA: Well, most artists would say that their life's work is all one work, and I think that is true. But I understand what you are saying. It's hard to know whether a building's design is the result of a new context that presents special challenges or whether it is a new piece of vocabulary developing.

MA: I should be more specific. In the Fort Worth building, the characteristics of containment and transparency seem very carefully balanced; that is, a concrete interior core surrounded by an *engawa* encased in glass. The Pinault building seems to have much more glass and as a result I would assume that the characteristic of transparency is more dominant. I'm not trying to get you to say that our building has perfect balance, but I am curious about the issue of holding space so that it is palpable to the visitor and does not completely escape out into the atmosphere, as it were. What were your thoughts in that regard in designing the Pinault complex?

TA: The Pinault building is a very large—some 60,000 square meters—museum of contemporary art. Most importantly, it's on an island in the River Seine, which is a central artery of Parisian life and culture. The challenge there is to reach out and connect to that life, and bring new energy to it, and at the same time create a protective structure for art. It's a very big challenge. Some of the architects who participated in the competition decided in the end not to engage it, and perhaps wisely. We are developing the models now and my approach, which has its contradictions, involves on the one hand not just creating a container, but a type of atmospheric image that stretches beyond itself, to be a spatial axis for the energy of the city. So the skin of the building will have aspects of reflection and translucency. The fact that it is on a river, however, makes it challenging in that regard. The issue of containment and protection are very important. Having water all around the building, and in some cases the river could begin to flood the island, made it essential that we protect the artworks inside. So the gallery spaces are actually raised above the ground level by about ten meters. Like Fort Worth, it is also a double-skin building, with an interior gallery space of protective museum walls with a glass skin placed outside of that. But here the glass is designed as a façade rather than an *engawa*. This façade will have qualities of transparency but also reflection. It's very thick glass—louvered glass that is about an inch thick—so it is more translucent than it is transparent.

MA: Did I read somewhere that you imagined it as a space ship?

TA: It could be like that; a form that is clearly defined, partly from reading the context of the shape of the Seguin Island itself, but at the same time suggesting motion or energy, hovering in a spatial axis.

MA: One of the themes that keeps coming up in our discussions over the years is the balance of protection and transparency in terms of creating form. Has that balance changed in any way since September 11th? In other words, is protection and security a more important issue for buildings than opening up to the outside world?

TA: I'm not sure it's appropriate to connect the September 11th tragedy directly to the physical issue of architecture. It seems hasty to jump to the conclusion that protection and security is the most important issue for buildings. The strongest buildings or even a fortress could not survive the attack of a jet airplane full of fuel. That tragedy provokes broader questions. We can never tolerate terrorism but we have to think about these tragic events more fundamentally. All I can do as an architect is consider the diversity of people on this planet and how architecture can help bring them together; not just as a meeting place, but a space of inspiration. As an architect, this is all I can do—to create a dialogue between diverse cultures, histories, and values. We can learn so much from each other and our past.

This book is published in conjunction
with the opening of the new Modern
Art Museum of Fort Worth, designed by
Tadao Ando, December 2002.

First published in 2002 by the Modern
Art Museum of Fort Worth in association
with Third Millennium Publishing Limited,
a subsidiary of Third Millennium
Information Limited
Shawlands Court, Newchapel Road
Lingfield, Surrey, RH7 6BL, UK
www.tmiltd.com

ISBN Museum's special limited edition
0-929865-19-7
ISBN Hardcover edition
1-903942-10-1

Edited by Susan Colegrove and Pam Hatley,
Modern Art Museum of Fort Worth
Designed by Peter B. Willberg
Produced by Third Millennium
Publishing, a subsidiary of Third
Millennium Information Limited
Printed and bound in Italy by Grafiche D'Auria s.r.l.

Library of Congress Cataloging-in-Publication Data

Ando, Tadao, 1941-
Seven interviews with Tadao Ando/
Michael Auping.
        p. cm.
    ISBN 1-903942-10-1 (alk. paper) -- ISBN 0-929865-19-7
    (special ed. : alk. paper)
    1. Ando, Tadao, 1941---Interviews. 2.
Architects--Japan--Interviews. I. Title: 7 interviews with Tadao Ando.
II. Auping, Michael. III. Modern Art Museum of Fort
Worth. IV. Title.
    NA1559.A5 A35 2002
    720'.92--dc21
                                        2002009571